Santa Clara County Free Library

REFERENCE

YOSEMITE

Half Dome, rising a sheer mile above the floor of Yosemite Valley, is virtually a trademark of the national park. On the preceding page is shown Upper Yosemite Fall.

THIS BEAUTIFUL WORLD   VOL. 16

YOSEMITE

by PAUL C. JOHNSON

with photographer

Thomas Tracy and others

197552

Published by

KODANSHA INTERNATIONAL LTD.

Tokyo, Japan & Palo Alto, Calif., U.S.A.

PHOTO CREDITS

Wallace Cathcart, half-title page, 6, 99, 101, 102, 106, 107;
Frances Coleberd, 57; Philip Hyde, 28, 30; Forrest Jackson, 24,
27, 55, 56, 72, 84, 85, 96; Paul C. Johnson, 2, 3, 7, 33, 47, 49, 50,
52, 53, 59, 60, 61, 62, 63, 64, 66, 77, 78, 86, 87, 88, 89; Dana
Morgenson, 32, 36, 37, 38, 39, 40, 45; National Park Service,
1, 4, 5, 8, 9, 31, 41, 43, 58, 68, 75, 76, 79, 82, 98; Oakland Art
Museum, 80; Betty Randall, 44, 46, 89; R. J. Santibanez, 48;
Thomas Tracy, front cover, frontispiece, 15, 16, 17, 18, 20, 21,
23, 34, 35, 42, 51, 65, 91, 92, 93, 100, 103, 104, 105, back cover;
Yosemite Park and Curry Company, 10, 11, 12, 13, 14, 19, 22,
25, 26, 29, 54, 67, 69, 70, 71, 73, 74, 81, 83, 94, 95, 97. Graphics
coordination and layout: Judith Whipple.

*Distributed in the British Commonwealth (excluding Canada and the
Far East) by Ward Lock & Company Ltd., London and Sydney; in
Continental Europe by Boxerbooks, Inc., Zurich; and in the Far East
by Japan Publications Trading Co., C.P.O. Box 722, Tokyo. Published
by Kodansha International Ltd., 2-12-21 Otowa, Bunkyo-ku, Tokyo,
Japan and Kodansha International/USA, Ltd., 577 College Avenue,
Palo Alto, California 94306. Copyright in Japan 1970, by Kodansha
International Ltd. All rights reserved. Printed in Japan.*

Library of Congress Catalog Card No. 71-117382
S.B.N. 87011-127-2; J.B.C. No. 0326-781516-2361
First edition, 1970

CONTENTS

1. *Early drawing* of Yosemite Valley romanticized the grandeur of the Sierran setting that awed the first visitors.

YOSEMITE

The first preserve in the world to be set aside for its scenic grandeur, the core of Yosemite National Park was created more than a century ago by an act of Congress, signed by President Abraham Lincoln on July 7, 1864. The law established Yosemite as a state park, comprising a fifty-square-mile grant that included the famous canyon and a grove of giant sequoia trees thirty-five miles to the south.

Because of its remoteness, Yosemite's discovery came late in the history of California. Spaniards, Mexicans, and the early Americans had occupied California for eighty years before the first white men stepped foot in Yosemite Valley in 1851. Others had probably sighted the gorge from vantage points on the rim earlier, but the evidence is inconclusive, and credit for the discovery is generally accorded to a party of militia who entered the valley in 1851 in pursuit of Indian raiders.

Prior to the 1850s, Yosemite was the home of the Ahwahneechee Indians who had summered there for decades, at peace with their neighbors and their surroundings. They occupied a score of permanent villages on the floor of the valley and temporary hunting encampments in the higher elevations. About four hundred were living in this mountain fastness when the Gold Rush brought thousands of prospectors to the Sierra Nevada and threatened to expose their idyll.

The secret was broken by the Indians themselves, who, finding settlers moving ever closer to their sanctuary, dispatched raiding parties to steal their goods and drive them away. A company of state militia, known as the Mariposa Battalion, was activated and sent to punish the raiders and herd the rebellious tribe into a reservation. It was this troop of cavalry in pursuit of the Yosemity Indians—as they were first thought to call themselves—that burst upon the magnificent panorama. Aware of the importance of their discovery, the troop named many of the features in the valley and named the valley itself for the Indians they were pursuing. Members of the expedition brought back awe-filled reports on the landscape they had found and stimulated venturous travelers to visit the region after the Indian danger had been neutralized.

For some of the firstcomers, the matchless beauty of the valley was less impressive than the resort potential it offered, and the valley soon became an object for commercial exploitation. Fortunately for posterity, its inaccessibility restricted the number of visitors to the doughty few and made commercial development difficult. As it was, the first tourist party reached the valley in 1855, two crude hotels were opened the following year, and toll horse-trails were blazed in 1856 and 1857. An enterprising young English forty-niner named James M. Hutchings began publishing a journal in 1856, *Hutchings California Illustrated*, that extolled the glories of Yosemite and prompted hundreds of readers to attempt the strenuous trip to the valley.

As visitors began to find their way into Yosemite in growing numbers, agitation was started to place the area under federal protection to preserve it for the benefit of all rather than for the lucky few. The campaign succeeded, and Congress granted the valley to California to administer, along with the 200-acre grove of giant sequoia trees to the south. The big trees were brought under protection because their existence was endangered by unbridled logging and exploitation as tourist curiosities. The legislation that set up the park was the first in a long train of bills that have over the years created the national park system, a conservancy unique in all the world.

Once the park was established, development picked up briskly. Wagon roads were completed to the valley in 1874. By 1878 there were nine hotels in the valley or on the rim, a public campground had been opened, and a telegraphic link with the outside world completed. After the transcontinental trains reached the approaches to the park in the 1870s, the railroads launched national advertising campaigns that drew thousands of excursionists.

Within a few years, it became evident that isolation of the two preserves was not sufficient in itself to insure their survival. Drainage basins above Yosemite were being overgrazed by thousands of sheep, destroying the high mountain meadows and causing spring floods in Yosemite and elsewhere. Furthermore, giant sequoias were still being felled throughout the Sierra. Under the prodding of a tenacious firebrand named John Muir, interested citizens persuaded Congress to expand the boundaries of the grant in 1890, creating Yosemite National Park, a 1,400-square-mile domain surrounding the original grant. The vastly increased acreage brought into the park not only the watersheds of the valley's rivers but a great mountainous preserve that included some of the finest scenery in the Sierra.

2. *Preview of Yosemite* Valley for▶
motorists arriving from the north is
this vista of the Gates of the Valley,
seen from an overlook high above the
plunging Merced River.

YOSEMITE ⁙

For several years, the state administered the small park engulfed
within the large one; then, in 1905, California re-deeded the
Yosemite grant back to the federal government for unified
operation. Administration of the national park, which had originally been entrusted to the U.S. Army in 1890, was carried on
by cavalry units until 1914, when a predecessor to the National
Park Service assumed the task.

When it finally came under central control, the national park
developed rapidly and sensibly. Roads were improved, a compre-
hensive trail system built, additional campgrounds opened, and
concessionaires brought under control. Most of the early operators
dropped away, leaving the field to two companies that eventually
joined as the present Yosemite Park and Curry Company.

Under a succession of dedicated superintendents, working with
an enlightened concessionaire and an understanding public, the park
service has been able to hold true to its challenging mission to
preserve the scenic wonders in their natural state for the enjoyment
of all, and is even now planning for progressive developments in
the future.

3. *Majestic Yosemite Valley* (*see overleaf*) was the▶
first scenic wonder set aside by government decree
for the benefit of all the people. This view from the
mouth of the Wawona Tunnel has mesmerized
travelers for more than a century.

4–5. *These gigantic trees* in the Mariposa Grove, older than Christianity, were brought under federal protection in 1864 by President Lincoln.

6. *High Sierra (see overleaf)*, John Muir's "Range▶
of Light," provides a heady mountain playground.

7. *Merced River*, which runs the length of the valley, is fed by a dozen waterfalls. It often floods in spring, then ebbs to a placid flow by autumn.

Incomparable Valley

"As I looked, a peculiar exalted sensation seemed to fill my whole being, and I found my eyes in tears with emotion." So wrote an awestruck member of the first party of white men to enter Yosemite Valley in 1851. The writer was a militiaman attached to the Mariposa Battalion in pursuit of marauding Indians; he did not have time to linger and admire the scenery. But his feelings have been shared by countless thousands in the hundred and twenty years since, and are felt today by each newcomer when he first views the grand panorama.

There are other stone-walled gorges in the country, but none seems to match the overpowering impact of this nine-mile-long valley between three-thousand-foot cliffs. The stark contrast between the eternal granite rising above a gentle living landscape of forest, meadow, and shimmering river evokes a religious response in many beholders, and more than one observer has likened the valley to a great cathedral.

Traditionally, the valley itself has been the principal magnet for travelers ever since the park was opened. "Yosemite" means "Yosemite Valley" to most people, and, even though the canyon comprises less than one per cent of the total area of the park, it attracts ninety-nine per cent of the tourists, and it is here that eighty thousand weekenders are prone to jam themselves on a Fourth of July.

The major resorts, stores, restaurants, visitor centers, camping facilities, and park service office are located here. It also has the heaviest concentration of spring and fall color, the largest quota of bear and deer. The combination of natural and man-made attractions is hard to resist. But people who know the valley well have learned that they can elude the crowds with little effort. Trails

19

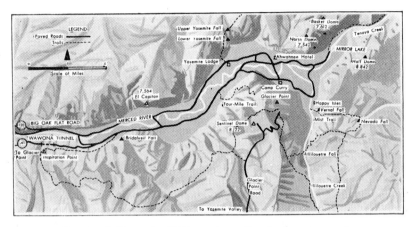

Dead-end Yosemite Valley, nine miles in length, a mile wide and nearly a mile deep, harbors the principal natural and man-made attractions.

along the river's edge or the base of the cliffs are surprisingly empty of people, and the stroller can often gain there the illusion that he is alone with the serenity of nature, despite the teeming presence of his fellows.

The park service and the concessionaire work hard to counteract the stifling charms of the valley and do their best to persuade visitors to head for other sections of the park. The campaign is moderately successful. Indeed, there are many old Yosemite hands who find the less crowded areas far more rewarding and rarely visit the valley. The time will doubtless come when motor vehicles, which now make the valley almost too accessible, will be banned and only passenger transports and bicycles will be seen on the roads—and the canyon may regain some of its pristine beauty.

What brought about this geologic extravaganza? For many

years, scientists argued two opposing theories on the formation of Yosemite Valley. One school held that a great cataclysm had elevated the Sierra and split open the mountains. A second group, championed by John Muir, who was regarded as a romantic upstart by the first school, advanced the hypothesis that the great chasm had been carved by glaciers during the Ice Age. The second theory eventually won out, for there is too much evidence of glacial action to be ignored. Granite surfaces glisten with the telltale sheen of glacial polish, erratics—rocks carried long distances from their points of origin—litter the high country, and the presence of active, though minuscule, glaciers further reinforces the glacial theory. At times, the Tuolumne River takes on a slightly milky cast from glacial flour, tiny particles of stone buffed off the mountainside by the grinding ice.

1. Yosemite Valley was once a V-shaped gorge cut by Merced River.

2. During the Ice Age, huge glaciers gouged it into U-shape.

3. After glaciers left, a lake formed and created level floor.

8. *Three Brothers*, a trio of matching rock formations, rise 2,000, 3,000, and 3,773 feet above the valley floor and are typical of the many rocks, spires, and shafts that edge the valley wall.

9. *El Capitan*, one of the world's ▶ largest rocks, rises 3,464 feet above the valley floor—two and a half times the height of the Rock of Gibraltar. Ranked an outstanding climb for mountaineers, it has been scaled several times by rock-climbing teams.

11. *Climbing team* on face of El Capitan is roped together for safety.

◄10. *Loaded with hardware,* climber inches his way along, holding on by toes and finger-tips.

12. *Climber negotiating* horizontal outcrop is held in place by nylon rope secured to steel pitons pounded into crevices in the granite. ►

13–14. *Spectacular ice cone* forms at the base of Upper Yosemite Fall during cold winters. Large chunks of ice on rock wall drop with the roar of a cannon shot when loosened by the sun's warmth.

15. *Renowned Yosemite Falls,* ▶ dropping 2,425 feet in three giant steps, are among the world's highest waterfalls. A roaring torrent in spring, they dwindle to a trickle in August, sometimes dry up. (*See Plate 59*).

16. *Most visible* and distinctive of the  Yosemite landmarks, 8,800-foot Half Dome can be seen from many points outside the valley. First scaled in 1873, the monolith has been climbed many times. Rock climbers ascend the steep facade (a two-day jaunt) and hikers scramble up the back with the help of a cable ladder.

17. *Bridalveil Fall* (620 feet) is one of the most beautiful and reliable of the valley's waterfalls. When all others are dry, diaphanous Bridalveil is still likely to be running. A brilliant rainbow forms in afternoon sunlight in the mist at its base.

18. *Mirror Lake* reflects Mount Watkins and Half Dome on days when there is no wind to ruffle its glassy surface. The shade cast on the lake by the surrounding mountains helps to create a perfect reflecting surface. The lake is at its best when brimfull in spring.

19. *Sunrise services* are held here in the nippy early hours of Easter. Since the sun does not rise over the lake until 9:30 in the morning, the service is a boon for late sleepers.

31

22. *Spectacular Vernal Fall,* ▶ easily reached from the valley, is a popular climb for hikers, who dry off on a sunny rock platform at the head of the fall. The 317-foot drop carries the full force of the Merced River and at flood stage will be 75 feet across. Rainbows form in the foaming mist at the base.

21. *Steep and slithery,* the trail has protective railings along its most difficult sections. Some hikers find the descent harder than the ascent, because of the muscular strain in holding back on the downslope.

20. *The Mist Trail* more than lives up to its name. Hikers are drenched by soaking spray from the falls.

23. *Nevada Fall*, second of the major waterfalls on the Merced River, is nearly twice the height of Vernal (594 feet vs. 317 feet). Because of the configuration of the cliff edge over which it pours, the water spurts into the air for a free fall onto the rocky basin below.

24. *Vernal and Nevada* Falls lie about three miles apart up the Merced Canyon. For twenty years (1870–90), a chalet stood in the flat between the two falls. La Casa Nevada was widely respected for the potency of its mountain dew.

25. *Bright blue rental bikes*, weaving along the shoulder, are a familiar sight. They offer a pleasant way for families to explore the flat valley.

26. *Swimming beaches* ▶ line the banks of the Merced where it meanders through the meadows. Farther west, the rocky channel is hazardous for swimmers.

27. *Children riding* a string of gentle burros saunter forth on a guided trip over the valley's bridle paths. Horseback parties also depart daily in summer for six-day loop trips through the High Sierra.

29. *Comfortable rooms* in the Lodge's motel-style resort are available in all seasons.

28. *Half camping*, half resort, con-
crete-walled tent cabins along the
river provide the benefits of both
types of housing.

30. *Luxury caravansary*, the Ahwah-
nee Hotel, a noble pile of boulders
built in 1927, ranks high among
the nation's resort hotels. It has a
short pitch-and-putt golf course
and it is the setting for a famous
Christmas dinner that attracts
diners from all over the country.

31. *Surprised* by an early snowfall, three does stand uncertainly in the mantled roadway. Snow does not remain on the ground long, so the valley's mule deer stay through the winter.

Swing of the Seasons

Unlike the well-advertised climate of California in general, the seasons in Yosemite march through four decisive periods, almost as pronounced as a New England calendar.

The coming of spring in Yosemite Valley is signaled by a dazzling floral display along the Merced River. Just west of the park entrance, redbuds burst into magenta fireballs. Within the park, dogwoods break into a mass of white blooms, echoed by the low growing azaleas and rhododendrons. Meadows turn to a rich green, brightened with splashes of blue lupin, scarlet paintbrush, daisies, and acres of yellow sneezeweed.

The first drowsy bears return from their long rest, the woods resound at dawn and dusk with the songs of mating robins, jays, juncos, and warblers. The waterfalls begin to gush forth as the snow melt reaches them, and scores of short-lived falls tumble down in unexpected places.

Summer comes on gradually. Heat builds up within the warming oven of the granite walls. Thunderheads tower above the rock wall in the afternoon and bring down brief, cooling, and highly localized showers. Wildflowers dry up, returning to seed for the long hard months ahead. The birds quiet down, busy raising their new broods. Animals hurry about the business of taking in food for the fall and winter. After dark, raccoons solicit the campers, and bears rummage through the largesse of the campground supplies.

Summer ends in a nervous aridity. The trails are dusty; trees are dry. Random electric storms pass over the park, cannonading in the granite echo chambers, kindling hundreds of small fires and decapitating tall snags with explosive force.

Fall comes in fits and starts. The first frosts, in late October, are followed by the bright fires of autumn. The majestic black

32. *Sign of spring*: redbud growing ▶
along the Merced River approach to
Yosemite flames into a puffball of
massed magenta blossoms.

SWING OF THE SEASONS ✿

oaks flare into great fountains of tawny gold, cottonwoods turn a
bright lemon yellow, and dogwoods add splashes of red.

Winter begins with the heavy downpours of November, followed soon by snow, which rarely remains in the valley for more
than a few days. Bears, squirrels, raccoons go into their winter
doze; deer stay around through the winter, and so does the coyote
chorus. Birds are silent and well-nigh invisible.

The seasons in the upper elevations are equally pronounced, but
linked to a different time cycle. Spring comes late to the high
country, which is either sealed in snow until June or so saturated
with ground water that flowering plants cannot get started.
Wildflowers that have long since dried out in the valley below
bloom at Lake Tenaya and later still at higher elevations.

The spring blooming period is incredibly brief, lasting only
two or three weeks. Wildflowers have at most eight weeks to run
through their whole life cycle—to sprout, form leaves, blossom,
and produce seed—before killing frosts hit around Labor Day.

Summer can be warm, even hot, despite the higher elevation,
but it is generally cooler than in the valley sun pocket below.
Brief thundershowers materialize swiftly, followed by sunshine
that makes the hail-littered highway steam.

Fall, a brief pause between the wet and dry seasons, is barely
discernible because of the absence of broad-leafed trees and shrubs
in the high country. Here and there, a pocket of quaking aspen
turns to shimmering gold, but most of the fugitive color comes
from ground covers. Acres of bilberry turn many a meadow into
a scarlet carpet for a few weeks. Comes the end of October and the
first snowfalls close down the year. Soon after, heavy storms
dump the deepest snow in the nation on top of the Sierra crest.

33. *Senecio* appears in forest meadows above the valley rim.

34. *Leopard or tiger lily* grows in wet meadows, from June to August.

35. *Lupine* is common in meadows and along roads throughout the park.

36. *Pacific dogwood* bursting into airy bloom in forested spots along the river announces spring in the valley. Shrubs grow to thirty feet in height.

37. *Western azalea*, a fragrant native, grows in moist meadows and alongside streams. It blooms in the valley for about a month.

40. *Summer flower show* in the High Sierra, a blossom-flecked meadow at Glacier Canyon (11,000 feet) is brightened by Indian paintbrush, yellow senecio, and corn lilies. Display lasts two to three weeks. ▶

38. *High country color*: red heather may be seen along the Tioga Pass in July above 7,500 feet.

◀39. *Pride* of the mountain is a common rock flower seen along the Glacier Point and Tioga roads in July.

41. *In summer*, mule deer are everywhere in evidence. Here, buck keeps company with his doting harem. He will desert them when the rutting season is over.

42. *Summer scroungers* in campgrounds below 5,000 feet, irresistible raccoons beg for food. Indiscriminate, they will eat almost anything, fingering the morsals delicately with their handlike paws.

43. *Black bears*, summer favorites of the touring public and bane of the park service, cadge handouts from tenderhearted tourists, despite repeated warnings against such indulgence. Once accustomed to human food, some bears become dangerous pests in their quest for man-made treats.

46. *Tawny gold* of the towering California black ▶
oaks provides the principal source of fall color in
the valley; it blends with the brilliant lemon yellow
of cottonwoods along the river.

44. *Fall color* en-
livens the water
where aspens grow
in damp areas.

45. *First harbinger*
of fall, the Pacific
dogwood turns a
bright red, the only
true red in the
valley.

47. *Most brilliant* flash of fall color in the valley comes from an American elm, sole survivor of a row set out in 1860 along a long-gone road.

50. *Winter (see overleaf)* casts a spectral spell over the Gate of the Valley, turning rocks and reeds into mysterious clumps of white.

48. *Black oaks, elm,* apple, and cherry trees combine to provide the Village Chapel (1879) with a New England air.

49. *Fall coloring* ▶ stages a romantic background for a November bride.

52. *Closed* for the winter. Heavy snow shuts down many park roads for six months of the year.

51. *Plow flings* freshly fallen snow to the treetops in an effort to keep the road open in winter. Three highways are plowed throughout the snowy months to accommodate a heavy volume of vacationing and skiing visitors.

57

◄53. *Black oaks* are turned to white filigree by wet snowfall, which ices every twig with sparkling frost.

54. *Ice skaters* skim over a large open-air rink operated by the concessionaire. Lessons, equipment, and elastic bandages are available here.

55. *Winter storm* (*see overleaf*) breaks up after dumping a heavy snowfall on the valley and the surrounding peaks. Fall is heaviest on the rim, lighter at lower and higher elevations.

56. *Glacier Point* offers two starry panoramas: man-made constellations in Yosemite Valley below, and the sparkling heavens above.

Breathtaking Glacier Point

Most popular of all the vista points on Yosemite's rim, Glacier Point (7,250 feet) is regarded as one of the great natural wonders of the world. From this lofty outlook, a viewer can choose between two panoramas—vertical or horizontal.

From the lip of the point, the visitor can clutch the railing and look straight down into Yosemite Valley, 3,250 giddy feet below. Or his eyes can sweep the horizon and take in a vast prospect of peaks, valleys, waterfalls, and forests receding to the snowcapped High Sierra. Two massive glacial canyons curve around the distinctive bulk of Half Dome and unite in the Merced Canyon below. Down one gorge tumbles the Merced River, dropping over a pair of waterfalls whose roar can be heard four miles away.

The name Glacier Point has puzzled scholars because it was applied in the 1860s, long before the glacial theory of Yosemite's origin had been accepted. It is now known that the glaciers that carved the immense valleys and shaped the peaks also sculpted Glacier Point itself, which was buried under seven hundred feet of grinding ice, but this was not recognized when the name was bestowed in 1868.

The point has been a popular tourist destination since 1871, when the first precipitous horse trail was built from the floor of the valley to the cliff top. This route, known as the Four-Mile Trail, has been in steady use ever since, with only a brief respite in 1929 for some re-engineering. Access to the point was increased by the opening of a wagon road in 1882 and a second trail, leading from Nevada Fall, in 1885. The toll road operated until 1917, three years after motor vehicles were permitted in the park, when it was turned over to the state. It was realigned and rebuilt in 1936, largely following the original route.

BREATHTAKING GLACIER POINT 🌿

Plans for a tramway up the east face of the point were prepared in 1887 but not acted upon for lack of funds. The idea has never completely died out, however, and it was recently reconsidered as one of several schemes for eliminating automobile traffic to the point.

The first hostelry to be built on the point, the Mountain House, was erected in 1878 and kept in constant use until 1969. In its later years, it was an engaging place to stay. The bedrooms, all located on the second story with a commanding view of the Sierra, were situated directly above the cafeteria and in the mornings were pervaded by delectable odors of coffee and bacon, drifting up through cracks in the floor. The historic building burned to the ground along with the nearby Glacier Point Hotel (built in 1917) in a brief holocaust one night in 1969.

To many tourists, one of the most enduring memories of Glacier Point is the famous fire-fall that operated off and on from 1871 to 1968. The production followed an established ritual. Watchers assembled at Camp Curry at the base of the cliff were admonished to be silent and at an appointed moment, a stentor at the camp bellowed the call, "Helllllloooooo Glllllaaaaccciiiier!" that drifted up the 3,000 feet and was plainly audible at the top. To this the firemaster roared back, "Helllooooo Caaaaammmmmmpp Cuurrrryyyyy!" Then came the command from below: "Llleeett theee fiiiirrre faaaall!" and the firemaster expertly pushed a half cord of burning fir bark over the cliff, forming a 1,000-foot streamer of sparks. This colorful tradition was discontinued by order of the park service, "as an artificial attraction incompatible with the national park idea of preserving America's wonders in their natural state."

57. *One of the most* photographed of trees, a Jeffrey pine on top of Sentinel Dome leans into the wind, twisted and stunted by its exposed site. In the forest, this tree would grow straight as an arrow.

58. *Yosemite Falls* can be seen in their entirety from Glacier Point or Sentinel Dome. Here, they are running in full flood, normal for late spring and early summer. By fall, they may be bone dry. (*See Plate 59.*)

59. *From Glacier Point* ▶ overlook, the floor of the valley looks like a view from an airplane. Visitors cling reassuringly to a railing that stands between them and the three-fifths of a mile of fresh air over an old apple orchard below.

60. *Half of* the stupendous panorama (*see overleaf*) visible from the point is the great glacier-carved Tenaya Canyon, presided over by Half Dome.

61. *Other half* of the sweeping panorama is the Merced Canyon, coursed

by the river that tumbles over Nevada
and Vernal Falls, four miles away.

62. *Alpenglow* suffuses Half Dome with a rosy hue, reflecting sundown tints in the eastern sky.

63. *Sunset casts* a fiery spell on the overlook, giving it the appearance of an embattled fortress.

64. *The Clark Range* takes on a softer character in the rays of the dying sun, which mellows the harsh geometry of the sculptured granite. Just beyond the dome-shaped Liberty Cap is Little Yosemite, a miniature carbon copy of the great valley.

65. *Nostalgic memory* for three generations of Yosemite visitors, the famous fire-fall bemused tourists off and on from 1871 until its discontinuance in 1968.

66. *Perspiring firemaster* at the top of the cliff pushed the embers over the rim with a long-handled blade. The fire dance called for daring, skill, plenty of muscle, and immunity from intense heat.

67. *On top* of Half Dome, across the canyon from Glacier Point, a team of Explorer Scouts stands on the brink of an overhanging ledge. With them, resting sensibly some distance from the edge, sits the first (and last) dog to climb this peak.

68. *How does Glacier Point* look from the top of Half Dome? Visible in the upper left are Glacier Point Hotel and Mountain House (both

burned down in 1969) and the steep cliff over which the fire-fall was pushed. Beyond: Sentinel Dome, Cathedral Peak, Merced Canyon.

69. *Cross-country* skiers swoop down fresh snow below Horse Ridge, near Glacier Point. Elsewhere, stakes mark out trails.

South to the Giants

South of the valley, a hundred-year-old highway rolls through a magnificent forest and covers in an hour's drive a span of contrasting interest ranging from a bustling ski area, through a nostalgic look at Yosemite's early days, and ending with a sobering confrontation with living things as old as the pyramids.

Key to the area is the Wawona Road, laid out in 1875, realigned at various times, and finally graded into its present high-speed surface in the 1930s. It was the first route to the valley, and for many years the main access from the nearest settlement, Mariposa. Staring out in 1856 as a toll trail ($2.00 per horse, one-way, $1.00 per walker), it ran several miles eastward of the present highway. An exhausting trip, the ride required forty saddlesore hours to get from Mariposa to the valley. After nine years of operation, it was replaced by the wagon road over which stagecoaches rocketed. A six-hour ride in a leather-sprung stage, through billowing clouds of dust, brought the passengers to Wawona; four more took them to the valley. The stages ran until 1917, when the motor car took over.

Leaving the valley on this road today is almost too easy. Fifteen miles south, a five-mile offshoot brings the traveler to the Badger Pass Ski Area, a milling spot on holiday weekends when several thousand skiers converge there from nearby cities in the Central Valley. In summer, the open bowl is a setting for a lavish concentration of wildflowers.

At Wawona (Indian name for big tree), a collection of early Yosemite buildings has been gathered by the park service in a pioneer history center. The dozen structures, some carried from remote locations in the park, have been painstakingly restored and furnished in the decor of their day. A covered bridge connects the

SOUTH TO THE GIANTS 🌿

village with an exhibit of wagons, including the fiendishly un-
comfortable stagecoaches that once bounced over the rocky roads.

Wawona Hotel, sprucely maintained by the park concessionaire,
dates back to the 1850s, when a predecessor lodge was built on its
site to serve travelers venturing out from the valley to see the big
trees or coming in from Mariposa. Bought out in 1874, the hostelry
burned down in 1878 and was replaced by the gingerbread buildings still standing and currently in use. A great favorite with
vacationers who find the valley too crowded and frantic, the hotel
faces an eighteen-hole golf course which sometimes has as many
deer as golfers roaming its emerald fairways.

Beyond Wawona, a spur road leads to the famous Mariposa
Grove, home of several hundred giant sequoias. Discovered in
1849, the big trees were brought under federal protection in 1864
along with Yosemite Valley, thirty-five miles to the north. The two
widely separated preserves were administered as a state park for
many years from headquarters set up in the grove. Later, when the
park boundaries were expanded into a national park and administration turned over to the army, cavalry patrols operated from a base
established on the site of the present Wawona Campground.

The majestic sequoias, once thought to be a form of redwood but
now known to be a different species, are often compared with the
coast redwood. Not as tall as the redwoods, the big trees are older
and more massive. Some are known to be over thirty-five hundred
years old. In the late 1800s, thousands were logged in the Sierra,
despite the fact that the lumber was too brittle for anything but
fence posts and shingles. The practice continued until 1890, when
the expansion of Yosemite and the creation of Sequoia National
Park sequestered the remaining groves.

70. *Midway between* Glacier Point and Badger Pass, a hostel at Ostrander Lake provides overnight shelter for skiers. It is usually well booked in advance.

71. *Easiest access* is sometimes through the second story window.

72. *Those who* do not relish overland skiing can ride a snowmobile to Ostrander and Glacier Point on one of its scheduled runs.

73. *Badger Pass* ski area is a popular ▶ destination for weekend skiers, with runs of graded difficulty, ski lessons, and packaged ski tours. Sometimes as many as seven thousand addicts will crowd the slopes on a holiday.

74. *Skiers unload* their gear at the entrance to Badger Pass ski lodge, nearly buried under a heaping snowfall. The lodge offers no overnight

accommodations but supplies refresh-
ments, a sunning deck, equipment
rental, and first aid facilities. The area
was opened in the 1930s.

75. *Wells Fargo Express* building is one of several historic structures restored in the Pioneer History Center at Wawona.

76. *Interior* of museum cabin is furnished in the authentic decor of its day. Each exhibit has a tape recording that tells the story at the touch of a button.

77. *Covered bridge* spanning the South Fork of the Merced River was built in 1857 and served continuously until 1931. Restored in 1961, it is the only covered bridge in a national park in the country. It connects the pioneer village with an exhibit of horse-drawn stages and freighters.

78. *Giant sequoias* in the Mariposa Grove tower above the log museum, replica of a cabin built in 1857 by the park's first custodian, Galen Clark. The enormous trees are little affected by fire or disease and live to great age.

79. *Famed attraction* in the grove was the Wawona Tree, through which millions of tourists rode. A tunnel was cut in its base in 1875, but the giant stood until felled by a snowstorm in 1969.

82. *The Grizzly Giant*, though not the largest tree in the grove, measures an impressive 96.5 feet around the base and soars to 209 feet.

80. *Extraordinarily* shallow root structure of sequoias is shown by this charming water color of the Fallen Giant, painted in 1878 by Lady Gordon Cummings.

81. *Sightseers' bus* transports visitors through the grove, now closed to cars.

83. *Bucolic Wawona Hotel* (*see overleaf*) is a favored resort for those who prefer a restful mountain retreat with a fine golf course. Little changed on the outside since the 1880s, the buildings are smart and modern inside.

84. *Tioga Road*, summer gateway to Yosemite, is
snowed in for half the year. Lake Tenaya, center,
becomes a sheet of ice in the winter.

Highway to the High Country

North of Yosemite Valley, a great scenic highway transects a vast wild land, half-forested, half-granite jumble, and offers the motorist a taste of a realm once the exclusive province of the hiking elite.

The road rewards travelers of all degrees of energy. It can be enjoyed by those who do not wish to leave their cars, by walkers who do not mind strolling a mile or two off the highway, and by the hardy few who abandon their cars in roadside parking areas for a week or two while they explore the wild lands afoot.

The route follows the modernized course of two old roads, once notorious for their hair-raising features. Leaving the floor of the valley, the motorist starts on a 1940 edition of an 1874 highway, the Big Oak Flat Road, originally built as a wagon approach to the valley. The old route, which followed a different grade up the canyon wall, was noted for its terrifying descent. The final five miles were too steep for stagecoaches and passengers transferred to horses for a ride so unsettling that, according to one passenger, "It is impossible to repress fear. Every nerve is tense; the muscles involuntarily make ready for a spring, and even the bravest lean timorously toward the mountain side and away from the cliff, ready for a spring in case of peril."

At Crane Flat, the modern highway joins another hoary old route, the Tioga Road, for a forty-five-mile run into the heart of the Yosemite High Country. This highway evokes painful memories from many present-day drivers, for as recently as 1961, some sections were little changed from the original mining road, haphazardly built in 1883. The narrow, rock-strewn path whipped in and out around trees and boulders, skirting precipices and clinging to the contours without benefit of cut or fill. Unfit for modern traffic, it was tardily replaced with the present spectacular roadway.

85. *O'Shaughnessy Dam,* accessible by a spur from the Big Oak Flat Road, backs up the Tuolumne River into a great canyon comparable to Yosemite Valley in grandeur. This gorge was the cause for a celebrated battle between conservationists and the city of San Francisco over the propriety of filling the canyon with water. As can be seen, the city won.

96

86. *On its climb* up the valley, Big Oak ▶
Flat Road passes the falls of Cascade
Creek, which roars down the moun-
tainside and under the highway

HIGHWAY TO THE HIGH COUNTRY 〰

There are many things to see along the way. A detour of sixteen
miles brings the traveler to O'Shaughnessy Dam and the Hetch
Hetchy Reservoir that fills a deep canyon comparable to Yosemite
Valley in grandeur. A one-way, down-only road—another memento
from the early days of road building and five-mile-an-hour speed
limits—picks its way through the Tuolumne Grove of giant
sequoias growing on a sloping site.

Here and there along the route, spur roads wander off to campgrounds a mile or two away, most of them set alongside trout
streams. As the road climbs into the granite country, every turn
reveals a new vista or a different view of the familiar peaks of
Yosemite Valley several miles to the south. For some distance, the
road passes through a veritable workshop of geology. Evidence of
mountain building and glacial action is close at hand, clearly cap-
tioned by interpretive plaques at turnoffs along the road. At one
point, the pavement strikes through a cut in an exfoliated dome that
was blasted open despite outraged protest from conservationists.

The highway crosses Yosemite Creek, rushing on its way to the
famous falls, skirts the shoreline of beautiful Tenaya Lake, crosses
wide-spreading Tuolumne Meadows, and then, at 9,941 feet, it leaves
Yosemite at the highest highway summit in the state and drops down
the steep eastern back of the Sierra to Owens Valley, descending
3,200 feet in thirteen miles.

Needless to say, this is a summer-only route. Deep snows seal
the pass from November through April, and may even close it
briefly before or after the winter season. As a consequence, the area
enjoys a very brief year, sometimes compressing spring, summer,
and autumn into three months.

87. *Several lakes* lie within hiking distance of the trans-Sierra road; some offer good fishing, but most of those above timberline are sterile.

89. *Quaking aspen*, growing in a hanging garden on the wall of the Grand Canyon of the Tuolumne, line a portion of the switchback trail down to Pate Valley from Harden Lake.

◄88. *Boulders* and reeds outline the shore of Harden Lake, an idyllic fishing spot north of the highway.

91. *Most accessible* of the high ▶ country lakes, Tenaya stretches for two miles along the Tioga Road. It is surrounded with granite domes, buffed into spherical shape by glaciers. Open to motorless boats, it is a popular sailing lake—the only one within the park.

90. *Popular site* for camping and picnicking, Tenaya was originally an Indian encampment and was named for the chief of the Yosemite tribe. The marshy area is noted for its large and sociable mosquitoes.

92. *Largest alpine meadow* in the Sierra, Tuolumne Meadows is enjoyed for its tranquil atmosphere and relative lack of crowds. A network of

trails radiates from the resort area,
leading down to Yosemite Valley and
up into the realm above timberline.
It is on the High Sierra Loop Trail.

94. *Rainbow trout* may be taken in the Tuolumne River during the season. Limits are set by the park service.

95. *Hiking party* on a guided excursion crosses a stream on a wobbly log. Both the park service and the Curry Company conduct field tours around the meadow and into the surrounding mountains.

93. *Jagged Cathedral Peak* (8,600 feet), chiseled by glacial action, is about four and one-half miles by trail from the Meadows. The precipitous granite sides provide excellent footing for rock climbers.

96. *Viewed* from Olmsted Point on the Tioga Road, the massive bulk of Clouds Rest seems to flow down into the Tenaya Canyon below, which passes Half Dome visible on the right. A stiff climb, the 9,000-foot summit offers a commanding view of almost the entire park. Deep cracks in the granite beside the highway indicate exfoliation, a step in mountain building.

97. *Overnight stop* on the High
Sierra Loop Trail, Merced Lake
Camp provides welcome food,
showers, and beds for the weary.

Hikers' Highland

Third world encompassed within the far-flung boundaries of the park is a highland of glistening peaks, mirror lakes, and flowering meadows approachable only on foot or horseback. This tranquil wild land is frequented by growing numbers of vacationers, some carrying all their worldly goods on their backs—food, clothing, shelter—some riding on astute trail horses.

This is the true High Sierra, a narrow band above 10,000 feet running for 200 miles down the spine of the Sierra, with the northern portion within Yosemite's boundaries.

Access is by a network of major and minor trails. Two major footways traverse the park. One, the famous John Muir Trail, built over a forty-year period, starts in Yosemite at Happy Isles and runs south, most of its path above 10,000 feet, ending at Mount McKinley 219 miles away in Kings Canyon National Park. The second artery is the Sierra Crest Trail that leads to the wild country to the north. Gateways to the trail system are in Yosemite Valley, Wawona, and Tuolumne Meadows.

Trails are carefully engineered, well posted with metal, bear-proof signs (bruin destroyed the earlier wooden ones), and easy to follow with the help of a topographic map. In early spring, however, some of the trails are barely negotiable. Icy rock prevents pack animals from gaining a footing; bridges, switchbacks, and trail markers may have been carried away by flooding. Hard-pressed trail crews do their best to repair the pathways, but often finish their work just in time for the onset of another winter. By the close of the short season, much of the limited forage has been grazed off by passing packtrains, and stock has to be pastured farther and farther away from camp.

The season is relatively short—June 15 to Labor Day—but

idyllic while it lasts. Newcomers to the region are struck by the absence of summer storms that permits camping out under a flawless sky for days on end. Their only complaint is likely to focus on the swarms of mosquitoes that infest some areas, bedeviling the backpackers until dark.

Hikers who are tired of lugging forty pounds of household goods on their backs can reduce their burdens by reserving accommodations at one or more of the six High Sierra camps operated by the Yosemite Park and Curry Company. Mostly situated below timberline in shaded swales, the camps offer minimal but most welcome facilities to the weary and footsore travelers. For that matter, hikers who balk at the idea of hiking can travel the same loop on horseback, thereby reducing their baggage to a toothbrush, a poncho, and a change of socks.

Today's hikers plodding serenely along the highland trails are perpetuating a mode of access that has changed little since Yosemite was discovered. The first visitors to the park walked or rode over trails such as these for two decades before wheels began to roll into the valley. The techniques for loading and cajoling a Yosemite pack mule have changed so little in the intervening century that an article on this manly art published in Hutchings's *California Illustrated Magazine* in 1859 is as appropriate today as it was then.

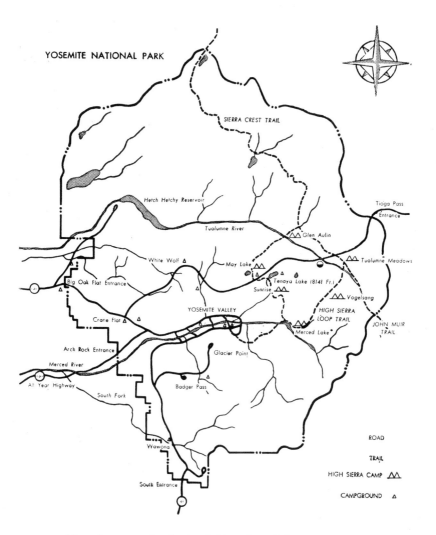

More than seven hundred and fifty miles of hiking and horse
trails thread the park, providing access to a great mountain
playground of streams, lakes, and peaks.

98. *Five small glaciers* still exist in Yosemite's high country. Here, a survey party slogs across the snow-covered ice of Lyell Glacier.

99. *May Lake* (9,300 feet), in the shadow of Mt. Hoffman towering 1,000 feet above, is the site of one of the six High Sierra Loop Camps. It is sometimes late in opening, as this Fourth of July scene suggests.

100. *High above timberline* (*see overleaf*), the sculptured granite landscape sweeps to the horizon like a frozen sea. Meadows form where lakes once sparkled, built up from the gradual accumulation of silt over the millennia. In this high land, grass grows sparsely, limiting forage for pack animals.

101. *Emerick Lake*, near Vogelsang, is an idyllic swale, offering ample feed for pack animals and natural bedding under campers' sleeping bags.

102. *Never at a loss* for words, Rye ▶ Krisp blares forth discordant comment on the day's proceedings—usually at daybreak when his human companions are enjoying their last blissful moments in the sack.

104. *Even in midsummer*, patches of snow may be found in the High Sierra, as at this 9,000-foot high lake photographed in August.

103. *Above timberline (see previous page)*, the rocky trails cross sunbaked regions as unfriendly as the moon. Hikers may have to go all day without replenishing water.

105. *Ice floes* in Jose-
phine Lake in April are
indicators of a heavy
winter and a delayed
spring. Trails are slip-
pery or boggy at this
season.

106. *Huddled together* for
warmth, a camping family
waits for the sun. Cold
spells in the highlands are
not uncommon in sum-
mer but are mercifully
brief.

121

107. *On the edge* of timberline, native and migrant trees struggle to adapt to gale winds, heavy snow, rainless summers, and little food in the sterile rock.